SUPER SPORTS STORIES

GRETA GUARDS THE GOAL

by Blake Hoena
illustrated by Christos Skaltsas

GRASSHOPPER

Tools for Parents & Teachers

Grasshopper Books enhance imagination and introduce the earliest readers to fiction with fun storylines and illustrations. The easy-to-read text supports early reading experiences with repetitive sentence patterns and sight words.

Before Reading

- Discuss the cover illustration. What do readers see?
- Look at the glossary together. Discuss the words.

Read the Book

- Read the book to the child, or have him or her read independently.
- "Walk" through the book and look at the illustrations. Who is the main character? What is happening in the story?

After Reading

- Prompt the child to think more. Ask: Greta is nervous to play goalie for her hockey team. Have you ever been nervous to try something new? What happened?

Grasshopper Books are published by Jump!
5357 Penn Avenue South
Minneapolis, MN 55419
www.jumplibrary.com

Library of Congress Cataloging-in-Publication Data

Names: Hoena, B. A., author.
Skaltsas, Christos, illustrator.
Title: Greta guards the goal / by Blake Hoena;
illustrated by Christos Skaltsas.
Description: Minneapolis, MN: Jump!, Inc., [2024]
Series: Super sports stories | Includes index.
Audience: Ages 7-10.
Identifiers: LCCN 2022048370 (print)
LCCN 2022048371 (ebook)
ISBN 9798885243858 (hardcover)
ISBN 9798885243865 (paperback)
ISBN 9798885243872 (ebook)
Subjects: CYAC: Anxiety–Fiction. | Hockey–Fiction.
LCGFT: Sports fiction. | Readers (Publications)
Classification: LCC PZ7.H67127 Gr 2024 (print)
LCC PZ7.H67127 (ebook)
DDC [Fic] –dc23
LC record available at https://lccn.loc.gov/2022048370
LC ebook record available at https://lccn.loc.gov/2022048371

Editor: Eliza Leahy
Direction and Layout: Anna Peterson
Illustrator: Christos Skaltsas

Printed in the United States of America at
Corporate Graphics in North Mankato, Minnesota.

For Vada and Mayim.

Table of Contents

Goalie Challenge

It's game day! Greta laces up her hockey skates.

"What position are you playing, Greta?" Samantha asks.

"It's my turn to be goalie," Greta grumbles.

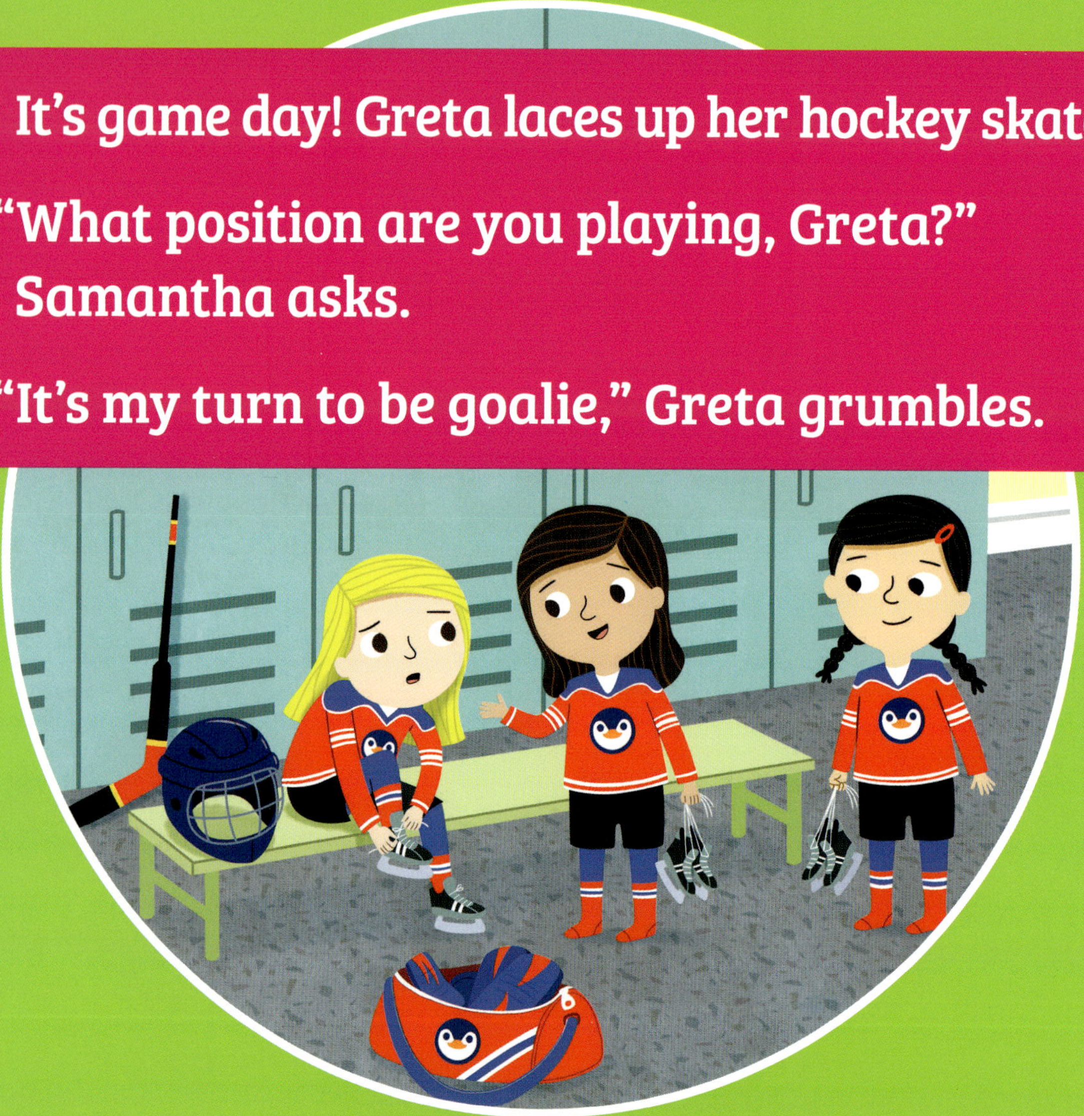

"Fun!" Li says. "I was goalie last game."

"I've never been goalie," Greta says. "I'm used to scoring goals, not stopping them."

"You'll stop lots of goals!" Samantha says.

"Greta, it's time to put on your goalie gear," Coach Kelly says.

Greta slips a glove on one hand and a blocker on the other. Coach helps her strap on the leg pads.

On the ice, the Penguins gather around Coach Kelly.

"Face-off is in five minutes, Penguins!" Coach Kelly says. "Let's try our hardest against the Hawks."

The team puts their hands in. They cheer. "Go Penguins!"

But Greta feels too nervous to cheer.

9
33
15

During warm-ups, the rest of the Penguins quickly zip around the rink.

Greta slowly skates to the goal. “I feel like a penguin,” she mumbles. “How am I supposed to save goals with all this gear on?”

15

Greta feels nervous as the centers line up for the face-off.

The referee drops the puck.

Whack! The Hawks get the puck.

Uh-oh! Greta thinks. *Please don't come this way!*

The Hawks' left winger passes it to their center as they skate toward Greta.

HAWKS
PENGUINS
0
0
15

The center shoots.

Thwack!

"Oh, no!" Greta shouts. The puck flies past her and into the net. Her stomach sinks. The Hawks are up 1 to 0.

"Good try!" Samantha says.

"Stick with it, Greta! You'll stop the next shot," Li says.

"I'll try my best," Greta mumbles.

The next time the Hawks have the puck, Greta gets ready.

I can do this! she thinks. *I will make my team proud.*

Greta watches as the Hawks' center passes to their right winger.

The right winger shoots.

The puck flies through the air.

Greta reaches out, and . . .

Smack!

She catches the puck in her glove!

"I did it! I did it!" Greta shouts.

"Great save!" Samantha shouts, skating over to Greta.

Li gives her a hug. "Isn't playing goalie fun?" she asks.

"Yes!" Greta replies. "I'm ready to stop more goals!"

Let's Review!

Greta plays goalie. What are the other positions on a hockey team? Where do they line up on the rink for face-off? Take a look!

1. **center:** The offensive player who usually does face-offs and scores goals.
2. **goalie:** The player who defends the goal.
3. **left and right defenders:** Players who help protect the goal.
4. **left and right wingers:** Offensive players who help the center score goals.

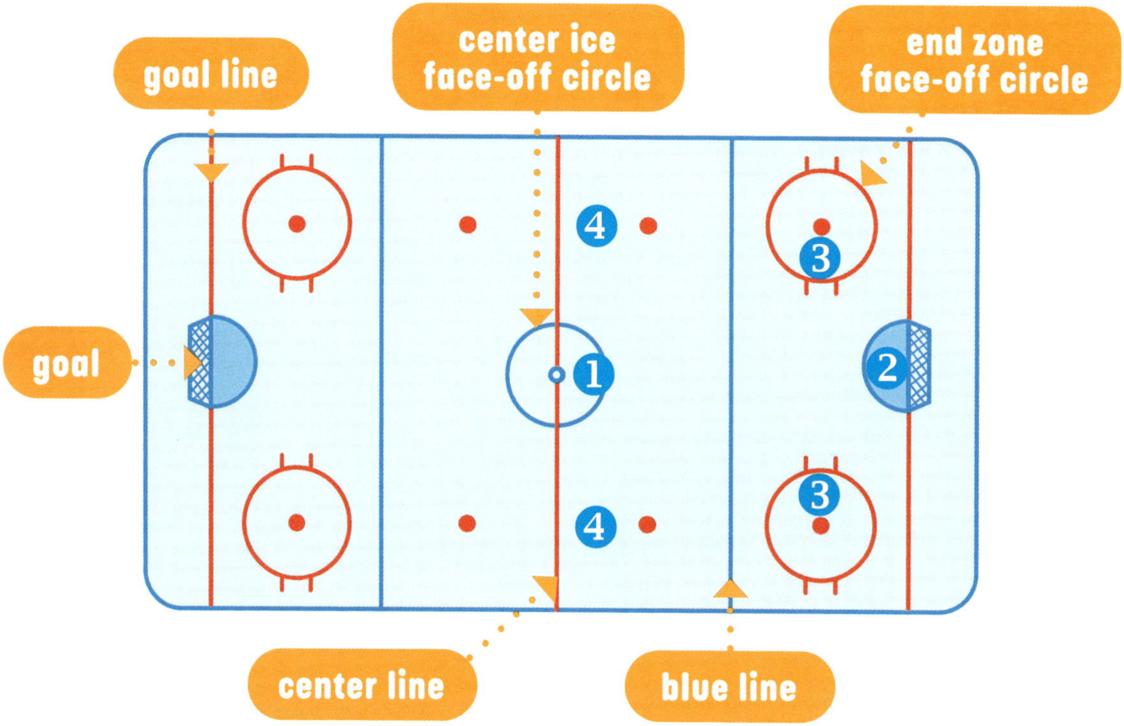

Hockey Equipment

What equipment does Greta need to play goalie? Take a look!

To Learn More

Finding more information is as easy as 1, 2, 3.

1. Go to www.factsurfer.com
2. Enter "**Gretaguardsthegoal**" into the search box.
3. Choose your book to see a list of websites.

Glossary

face-off: When a referee drops the puck to start a hockey game.

gear: Equipment or clothing.

laces: Ties a shoe or piece of footwear.

position: A particular role on a team.

puck: A hard, round, flat piece of rubber used in ice hockey.

referee: An official who supervises a sports match or game and makes sure players obey the rules.

warm-ups: A set of exercises done to get ready to compete.

Index